100 INSTANT IDEAS FOR ALL-AGE WORSHIP

By the same author:
100 Instant Children's Talks

100
Instant Ideas for All-Age Worship

SUE RELF

KINGSWAY PUBLICATIONS
EASTBOURNE

First published in Great Britain 1998
Reprinted 1999

ISBN 0 85476 763 0

Designed and produced by Bookprint Creative Services
P.O. Box 827, BN21 3YJ, England for
KINGSWAY PUBLICATIONS
Lottbridge Drove, Eastbourne, E. Sussex, BN23 6NT.
Printed in Great Britain.

Contents

Introduction

My purpose in writing this book is to provide a resource rather than a manual. The church of Jesus Christ comprises a multitude of different people, different situations and different contexts. No two local situations are alike. The ideas here will need to be selected and adapted to suit. How and when you use them is up to you!

Before attempting to plan all-age worship, it is helpful to ask the all-important question: 'What are we doing this for?' One answer might be: 'To take the opportunity to present simply and clearly the Christian gospel to visitors, particularly those who are parents'; another answer might be, 'To provide an opportunity for the church family to worship together and to nurture a sense of belonging'; or a further answer to this question might be, 'To give the children's workers a rest!' (This perfectly valid reason needs to be acknowledged. Plan a service which will build up and encourage children's workers.) Try to be as specific as possible. It is possible to have more than one aim, but it is important not to try to have too many. Once the aim or aims have been agreed upon, consider a second question: 'How can we best achieve this purpose at this time and in this situation?'

Answers to these questions will influence the planning

process. Themes and items will be carefully chosen to contribute to the overall purpose. Nothing will be included simply because it is deemed to be 'a good idea'. Focus is very important.

All-age worship usually provides an opportunity to try out something a little different. In fact, something a little different is usually what is expected. All-age worship presents an ideal opportunity for the church family to enjoy some wholesome activities together which are not normally associated with 'church'. God often uses the unusual and the different to speak and work.

However, 'all-age' does not mean 'childish'. It is important to avoid the temptation to use childish or patronising language when leading all-age worship. Having people of all ages together for any length of structured time is a challenge. Try not to have a bias to the youngest end of the spectrum, but on the other hand, the presence of children should not be ignored for too long. One or two items designed just for children can be included while adults watch or wait. Generally, items chosen should be accessible and meaningful to the majority. Spiritual truth presented briefly, simply and clearly edifies, instructs or convicts everyone.

Be filled with the great creative Holy Spirit as you plan, prepare and lead all-age worship in your church setting!

Mini-Talks

The ideas included in this section are mini-talks and are intended to be used as thought-provokers. They can be used to introduce themes or talks. They can be used to 'fill in' spaces or connect different parts of a service. They can be used to inspire worship or prayer. Or, they can be used in assembly-type situations where only a short talk is required.

1

Hebrews 1:3 says that Jesus sustains all things by his powerful word. He has the whole world in his hands.

Prepare a carrier bag filled with a variety of objects, both large and small, which can be carried.

Choose two volunteers. This is a good opportunity to choose a parent with their child if they are willing to volunteer together. Ask one volunteer to take the objects from the carrier bag one by one, and pile them up onto the other volunteer without any of them falling onto the floor. Those of us who remember *Crackerjack* on television will remember this game.

When the amazing feat has been achieved, or an object has been dropped, talk about how God carries the whole world in his hands, and never 'drops' anything. He is infinitely vast and powerful. Read Hebrews 1:3 if desired.

2

God is not confined to time as we are. The Bible clearly tells us that he is eternally God (Ps 90:2; 93:2).

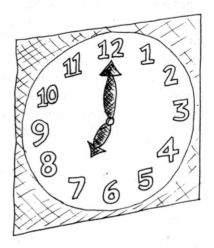

You will need a cardboard clock face with movable hands (attached with a paper fastener), a flash-card with your date of birth written on it and a flash-card with the current year written on it.

Begin by asking if anyone has the time right now. Then ask what the time was when the first person arrived. How much time has gone by? Then remark how amazing it is that for God himself no time at all has gone by. He is eternal. Use the clock to demonstrate how much time has passed.

Ask if anyone would like to guess in what year you were born. When someone gets it right, show the card with your date of birth and ask someone to work out how old you are.

Perhaps someone can work out the exact number of years, months and days. For God, it is as though no time at all has gone by. He will never grow old, nor has he ever been young. He is eternal.

Finally, ask the name of the current year. It is given a number. Show this flash-card. Does anyone know why this year has this number? It was thought that Jesus was born in the year '0' (in fact, he was born a few years earlier than that). Although all those hundreds of years have gone by since Jesus was born, for God no time has gone by. He is exactly the same. Unlike us, he does not live in a world where time goes by. He is outside time. It is hard to imagine it, but God has always been and will always be and he never changes.

3

God never gets tired and moody like we do. He is always present, always reliable, always the same (Ps 121).

Ask everyone to stand up and put one arm in the air, then lower it and raise their other arm. Lead everyone in raising their arms up and down like this together in rhythm. It is actually quite tiring, and your arms will start to ache after a while. (Choose a more energetic exercise if you want to tire the congregation more quickly.)

Ask those who are tired to own up. A few determined youngsters will want to keep going, so allow them to continue for a few more minutes.

Then explain that the Bible tells us that God never gets tired or goes to sleep. He is always there, always reliable and always awake and 'on the ball'. He never makes a mistake. Ask volunteers to look up Psalm 121 and find the verses which tell us that God is always awake. He is forever looking after us and caring for us. We never catch him off guard.

4

Job 31:4 tells us that God knows every step we take. The love and mercy of God for each of his children is beyond comprehension.

Choose two or three people of different sizes and ask them to walk round the perimeter of the room, counting the number of footsteps they take in one circumference. Compare their answers. Perhaps someone could walk round with a toddler and count their footsteps.

Apparently the average person takes about 18,000 steps every day! Think of a toddler or young child running about and how many steps they must take every day. Suggest that each person thinks about their average day and how much walking or running they do. Imagine God knowing every step! Read Job 31:4 together.

God knows every step we take. He knows everything we do. He is always watching over us.

5

There is no limit to the power of God. There is no limit to his knowledge, and his presence fills everything.

Prepare three large separate flash-cards with the words 'omnipresent', 'omnipotent' and 'omniscient' written on them.

Show each of the flash-cards in turn, asking a different

volunteer to try to pronounce each one. Practise pronouncing them together. Then ask if anyone can guess what each one might mean. Once the words have been explained, test the children to make sure they have learned the different meanings. Ask which one means 'knows everything there is to know', or 'is everywhere there is to be', or 'can do everything' several times.

Who is omnipresent, omniscient and omnipotent? Of course the answer is God. There is no one else like him. He is special, unique and wonderful. He is bigger and greater than we can imagine.

If you know it, sing the song 'God is so good', but substitute the words with 'God is omnipresent . . . he is everywhere', 'God is omniscient . . . he knows everything' and 'God is omnipotent . . . he is mega-powerful'.

6

God remembers everything. Nothing slips his mind; no small thing goes unnoticed. No person's life is too short or insignificant to be unseen by God. He even sees what happens to every single sparrow (Lk 12:6).

Choose twenty small and unusual items and place them in a cardboard box.

Take the items out of the box one by one, and show them to the congregation. If preferred, place each of them on an overhead projector where just their silhouettes will be seen. Next, tell the children present that you are going to show them all once more, except for one item. Do this, and then ask if anyone can tell you which item is missing. Repeat the exercise if desired.

Although our memories can be exceptionally good, God's

memory is beyond description. Read Luke 12:6 together. His knowledge is infinite. He notices everything. Nothing escapes his attention, and he is full of compassion for his children.

7

So often the things that fill our minds are trivial. God has told us what is most important, and it is vital that we agree with him.

Prepare two signs, one reading 'yes' and the other 'no'.

Prepare questions for the children to answer. Tell them they will need to think carefully about whether the answer should be 'yes' or 'no'. Ask them to call out one or the other. They are to say 'yes' if they think something is very important, and 'no' if they think it is not very important.

Examples of questions are given below. Show the signs 'yes' or 'no' according to the children's answers.

- Is it important to feed your pet?
- Is it important always to let someone know where you are?
- Is it important to eat good food?
- Is it important always to tell the truth?
- Is it important to get to school on time?
- Is it important to keep your toys tidy?
- Is it important to wear two socks that are exactly the same?
- Is it important to have neat hair?

There may be differences of opinion on some subjects! Choose questions which are relevant to your children's situations and round off by asking, 'Are some things more important than others?' The answer to this question is obviously 'yes'. Ask the children to name some things that they think are most important.

What did Jesus say was the most important thing of all? Can anyone think what it might be? Look up Mark 12:29–31 for the answer.

8

This short demonstration illustrates how things change when we pray to Jesus and invite him to take charge of situations in our lives. God is all-powerful and infinitely good. Nothing is too hard for the Lord (see Genesis 18:14).

Fill a tall clear tumbler half-full with water. Add one tablespoon of bicarbonate of soda and stir. Add two or three sticks of uncooked spaghetti broken into 3cm lengths. Stir for a few seconds. The water will slowly clear and the pieces of spaghetti will sink to the bottom. Add vinegar a little at a time to the mixture until the glass is nearly full. The vinegar causes a froth when it is first added, but this soon settles down. The pieces of spaghetti start rising up and down in the mixture after a short wait.

Adding the vinegar to the water changed things for the spaghetti. This is a simple picture of how Jesus changes situations for us in surprising ways when we pray to him and then wait in faith.

9

This very quick exercise can be useful to encourage every-one to remember that they are very important to God.

The Bible clearly tells us that everyone who believes that Jesus Christ is the Son of God and has received from him forgiveness for all their sins is a son of God (with a small 's'). In the Bible such people are called 'saints'. The word in English has become associated not with Christians in general but with exceptionally good people in particular. The word 'Christian' is only used very occasionally in the New Testament. It was a term coined by unbelievers to describe believers. The word the early Christians used to describe themselves was 'saints'. (See Philippians 1:1; 4:21–22.)

Have available a supply of address labels and give out one label to each person, with a pen if needed. If preferred, partly stick one to the underside of each chair in advance. Ask each person to write on the label 'St' followed by their name, and then wear the label. As far as God is concerned, we are all saints!

10

This idea is to remind everyone of how God is totally infinite in his understanding and knowledge. He blows our minds!

If desired, ask a volunteer to write the following huge numbers on an overhead projector.

Look up Psalm 139:13–14. These verses tell us that God was involved in our conception, development and birth. Apparently, the human body is made up of 10 trillion highly specialised working parts. Ten trillion is a one followed by nineteen noughts. Can you imagine it? Inside each of our brains are one million million nerve cells. One million million is a one followed by twelve noughts. Can you imagine it?

Look up Psalm 147:4–5. These verses tell us that each individual star is named by God. No one knows how many stars there are. No one has seen an edge to the universe – it seems to stretch on for ever in all directions. There are so many billions of stars that it is impossible even to guess how many there are. The Milky Way, which is only one of several thousand million galaxies, has an estimated 100,000 million stars alone. One hundred thousand million is a one followed by eleven noughts. Can you imagine it?

Look up Psalm 104:24. God has made everything in the world. The atom is the building block that God has used to make everything. Atoms are so small that 1,000 million together would be about the size of a full-stop. One thousand million is a one followed by nine noughts. Can you imagine it?

God is the God of the vast and huge. He is the God of the minute and small. He is the God who knows and loves every single human being.

11

A day is coming when God will judge everything and everyone. No single incident will be overlooked, and no single person will be unjustly treated. God's judgement will be totally fair and totally righteous. We cannot imagine how this could possibly be so, when the affairs of men are so complex.

Bring along a jam jar, with its lid on, filled with water. Place it on a table covering a postage stamp. Ask a volunteer to come and look at the jar and, without moving it, tell you what is underneath. The stamp will be invisible. When the lid is removed from the jar, the stamp becomes clearly visible through the water.

God sees everything that happens, all through time and in every place. Nothing escapes him. He sees a person's innermost thoughts and motives. We so often make our judgements knowing only half of a story.

Select one or two of the following Bible passages to read: 1 Samuel 16:7; Psalm 33:13–15; Psalm 96:10–13; Luke 12:6.

Praise and Worship

There is a tendency to think that all-age services mean children's action songs. Actually, although excellent for children-only groups, children's action songs were not written for adults. They do not provide a vehicle whereby older people can truly worship God from the bottom of their hearts. For this reason I prefer to use adult songs which declare God's praise in a simple, straightforward way, rather than ones which were written particularly for children. I have found that children survive quite happily for the first fifteen minutes of a service if there is plenty to interest them later, and adults feel happy participating in all-age type activities if they have first had an opportunity to worship God in a meaningful way.

The ideas which follow can be used as part of a continuous praise time, or interspersed with other ingredients and used as single items during the service.

12

Choose a psalm of praise, such as Psalm 66:1–5, and put the words into practice. After reading the verses through together, prepare to do exactly as it says!

Verse 1 says: 'Shout with joy to God, all the earth!' Prepare some phrases to be used as 'shouts of joy', such as 'I'm so happy I belong to you, Lord', or 'You are such a great God', or 'The Lord has made me glad to be alive'. Either choose one or two individuals to shout them out, or ask the whole congregation to shout them out aloud together.

Verse 2 says: 'Sing the glory of his name; make his praise glorious!' Choose a suitable song of praise to sing together.

Verse 3 says: 'Say to God, "How awesome are your deeds! So great is your power that your enemies cringe before you."' Ask everyone to say the words of this verse together.

Verse 4 says: 'All the earth bows down to you; they sing praise to you, they sing praise to your name.' Ask everyone to kneel down in honour of God as they sing together another song of praise.

Verse 5 says: 'Come and see what God has done, how awesome his works on man's behalf!' Ask those who know that God has done an awesome thing in their lives to stand up as a way of saying, 'Come and see what God has done.' If desired, ask those who are standing to say in one or two sentences what these 'awesome works' are.

There are several other psalms which can be used in this way, such as Psalm 81:1–3, Psalm 95:1–7, or Psalm 100.

13

Take the congregation on a journey in their imagination to the throne of God. Do this by asking everyone to close their eyes and imagine themselves walking along a very wide pathway, with lots of friends. Ask them to imagine lots of excited chattering going on. Then ask them to imagine the path leading through woodland and by a stream, and then narrowing as it goes uphill. As the hill gets steeper the pathway becomes narrow so that everyone starts to walk in single file, and realises that they are climbing up alone. As they reach the top of the hill a magnificent and enormous white building appears in front of them. It has huge wooden doors. The doors are closed, but each individual walks on towards them, and as they approach, they see the doors open. Jesus himself is standing there, waiting to welcome each individual. Smiling, he leads each person through the doors and accompanies them inside, to where God himself is sitting on his magnificent throne. God sees each one who arrives, and speaks to each person by name. Then God says, 'What is it you would like to say to me?'

Have a moment's silence at this point, so that each person can say to God what is on their hearts, and can listen to him as he answers.

14

The following is a useful and fairly quiet worshipful activity for children to do while the adults do something else.

On a long length of paper, or on the back of a roll of wall-

paper, write in large bubbly letters 'Praise the Lord' or 'We are God's children', making sure that the words contain more individual letters than the number of children who would be involved. Cover narrow tables with newspaper and lay the prepared length of paper on top. Ask the children to stand around both sides of the table and decorate one letter each. Provide glue, spreaders, scissors and aprons. Also provide a number of items which are suitable for collage, such as milk-bottle tops, polystyrene packaging, scraps of ribbon and tissue paper, pieces of old birthday wrapping paper, silver paper, etc. The children can hold it up and show everyone else when it is finished.

15

Choose a song which has several separate verses and instruct everyone, as each different verse is sung, to sit, then kneel, then stand, and finally raise their hands. Choose positions which suit the content of each verse.

16

While singing a song or hymn, part of which makes a request to God, such as 'Spirit of the living God', or 'Shine,

Jesus, shine', ask a section of the congregation to pray for the same request in their own words while everyone else sings. Choose sections of the congregation to sing and others to pray as the song unfolds, or sing the song through several times, so that everyone has a turn to pray and to sing.

17

Make available a long strip of white paper, or use the back of wallpaper. Lay it on top of a narrow table or tables, with a selection of felt-tipped pens nearby. Ask people to come to the table in twos or threes, and then draw or write on the paper something for which they would like to give thanks to God. Do this during the singing of a suitable song or hymn if desired.

When everyone has had a turn, ask some children to draw decorative circles and lines around all the individual thanksgiving drawings and prayers, joining them together. Then show the finished article to everyone and offer it to

God as a thanksgiving in prayer. Alternatively, ask for volunteers to hold it up while you sing a song of thanksgiving together.

18

In advance, ask one or two children or adults to choose a song which they would like to sing. Then, before it is sung, ask them to say briefly what it means to them and why they chose it.

19

Prepare a length of paper with the following written on it in large decorative letters: 'We really want to thank you for everything, Lord.' Lay it on a narrow table and have a selection of felt-tipped pens available. Ask the congregation to come to the table in twos or threes and draw a simple picture of themselves in or around the words. In doing this, everyone adds their 'signature' to the sentence and agrees with it.

20

When a baby starts to cry during a service, ask the parent to come forward with the crying child. Above the noise(!) turn to Psalm 8:2, which says: 'From the lips of children and infants you have ordained praise.' The Bible says that this baby is praising God! How can this be? The very fact that this baby can cry means that he or she is very much alive. Every new life is an incredible and unique creation of God, and apart from him it would not exist at all. Therefore this cry is as much praise to God as all the prayers and songs that older ones say and sing.

21

As we all know, toddlers can be noisy and do not always (if ever) want to sit still! Because of this they tend to be thought of as a problem in church services. Nothing could be further from the truth. The Bible tells us that children must be instructed and corrected, and this includes toddlers. But toddlers are eager to explore and play, and this natural instinct is God's idea!

Choose an appropriate point to turn to Zechariah 8:5. This verse says: 'The city streets will be filled with boys and girls playing there.' It is very relevant to boisterous toddlers and church! 'Boys and girls playing' are the promise of God's blessing. The city referred to in this verse is, of course, Jerusalem. In the New Testament God's holy city Jerusalem is likened to the church. So, this verse tells us that children playing happily are part of the church, and by virtue of being themselves, toddlers are a praise to God, and a sign of his blessing.

Prayers

The ideas in this section are given to encourage reality in our praying. They are to help young and old, those who are new to the Christian faith and those who are old-timers, to reach out in faith to the God who loves them. He loves us so much that he promises to respond to our prayers.

22

Give each person a piece of paper and a pencil, and ask them to write (or draw) something which they have really appreciated during the past week and want to thank God for. When everyone is ready, ask them to lay their paper on the palm of their hand and 'offer' it up to God.

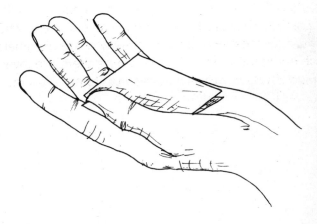

This idea can be developed in several ways:

23

After everyone has written or drawn their 'thank you', the pieces of paper can be collected in a basket, rather like the money offering, and then offered to God as a 'thank offering'.

24

Everyone can be asked to fold their pieces of paper, which are then collected in and redistributed. Each person can then take it in turns to read out the thanks of someone else. If there are too many people present to make this feasible, divide everyone into small groups or pews to read them out, or have a time of silent prayer.

25

Prepare a large cardboard box with a notice like 'We thank you, Lord, for one another' taped to the front. Ask everyone to write the name of someone they really appreciate and would like to thank God for on their piece of paper. Then ask everyone to come and drop their piece of paper in the cardboard box.

26

Ask everyone to write a personal prayer request on their piece of paper. When they have all done this, ask them to hold their 'request' tightly in their hand, holding it up as though they were giving it to God. A sentence such as 'We bring our prayers to you, our loving heavenly Father' can be said together as this is happening.

A passage of the Bible, such as Matthew 6:25–34, can be read at the same time.

27

Ask everyone to pray first for the person sitting on the right of them, and then for the person on the left. This can be done with a particular topic in mind, such as 'faith', 'boldness and confidence', 'personal needs', or 'spiritual growth'. Pray together silently, quietly or loudly, using prepared words if desired.

28

Divide everyone into pairs, and ask each pair to pray for each other. If desired, prepare a given phrase such as, 'Dear heavenly Father, I pray for your blessing to rest on. . . .'

29

Ask everyone present whose birthday is between January and March to stand. Everyone else is to remain seated. Ask those who are sitting to pray for those who are standing. Continue in this way through the months of the year until everyone present is prayed for.

30

Ask the men and boys to stand while the women and girls remain seated and pray for them. Then ask the women and girls to stand while the men and boys pray for them.

31

Ask everyone present who lives in a nearby street to stand. Everyone else is to pray for the people standing, and for the others who live in that street. Any method of praying can be used, such inviting people to repeat a prepared sentence, asking everyone to pray together in silence, or asking everyone to pray aloud at once. A different street can be targeted each week, or the whole congregation can be prayed for street by street, depending on the time available.

This idea can be developed in several ways:

32

Read out a list of the streets in the nearby area one by one, asking a representative of each street to come forward as the list is being read. Next, pray for each of the streets represented.

33

Prepare a large, simple map of the nearby area and display it. Ask each person or family to put a brightly coloured cross onto the map to represent their house. If this would take too long, then use several maps to represent different areas, or ask people to do this during the singing of a hymn or song. Next, pray for the whole area.

34

Churches in the area can be marked on a similar map in bright colours, and the Christian witness in the area can then be brought to God in prayer.

35

Ask each child who plays or goes to school in the nearby area to come forward. Ask the congregation to pray for the schools represented. Teachers or students can be prayed for in a similar way.

36

Ask everyone who is self-employed or who has responsibility in a local business to come forward. Ask some children to circle round each person who has come forward and to pray for God's blessing on them and their business.

37

The floor area of the room/tent/hall you occupy can be visualised as a map of your area or town. Corners of the room then become districts, and the middle becomes the town centre. Ask everyone to position themselves on the 'map', standing in the area or district in which they live. Those who are grouped together can then pray for their own neighbourhood.

38

Choose a recent local newspaper and cut out articles which are of interest. Divide everyone into small groups and give each group one of the articles. Ask them to pray for the people or situations which are mentioned.

This idea can be developed in several ways:

39

Choose a national newspaper, divide people into small groups and distribute chosen articles. Ask each group to pray about the issues mentioned.

40

Cut out short articles from Christian magazines, missionary magazines, or the magazines of relief organisations. Again, divide everyone into small groups and give each group one of these articles. Ask the groups to read and pray about these situations.

Alternatively, each group can be given a copy of a letter, or a section of a letter, which has recently been received from any absent members or missionaries. Each small group can then pray for the items mentioned.

41

Display the Lord's Prayer (Mt 6:9–13) on an overhead projector, or ask everyone to look it up in a Bible. Ask each person to consider which phrase or line they feel is the most appropriate for them at the present time. Say the prayer together, and ask each person to stand up as the line they have chosen is read out. They should then remain standing.

Explain that as this is the prayer Jesus himself taught us to pray, then God is committed to the sentiments which are expressed, and will surely answer each request.

At the end of the prayer, when everyone is standing, say the prayer again confidently together.

42

Choose some volunteers who are willing to sigh as loudly as they can. Who can make the most convincing and loudest sigh? Next, ask them to practise cheering. Who can make the loudest cheer? Talk about sighs and cheers. Are they different from words? They express our feelings.

Have prepared a list of prayer requests and a list of items for thanksgiving and praise. As you read out the list, ask everyone to 'feel' rather than 'think', and ask the volunteers to lead the congregation in either sighing or cheering as appropriate after each item is mentioned.

43

Halfway through a service, in the middle of any item, song, talk or announcement, interrupt abruptly and say, 'Stop!' Ask everyone what they have on their minds right now. Some will have been concentrating on the matter in hand, others will have been miles away. Give everyone a minute to pray about whatever was on their mind. God is interested in everything we are interested in. 'He cares for you' (1 Pet 5:7). Continue with the proceedings.

44

Read the Beatitudes one by one (Mt 5:1–10), leaving a time of silence after each one is read. Ask each person to consider during the silence their own character and habits in view of the qualities which are highlighted in these verses of the Bible. Then read out the verses a second time, pausing after each verse in the same way. This time ask the congregation to use the silence to ask God to impart to them that particular quality of character.

45

Cut out a selection of typical advertisements from glossy magazines. Prepare photocopied acetates to display them one by one on an overhead projector, or show them and describe them. Explain that 'idolatry' is a word in the Bible which God uses to describe attitudes that consider anything or anyone more important than God himself. God is great, unique and good, and he made every single person in his own image in order to enjoy a relationship with them. Idolatry, therefore, is like kicking God in the teeth, and is the worst sin of mankind.

Our advertisements are a reflection of the things in our culture which we value highly. They reflect society's priorities. Priorities determine actions.

Divide everyone into small groups and give each group one of the advertisements. Ask each group to compose a prayer of repentance based on their advertisement. Ask a representative of each group to read out their prayer in turn.

Bible Readings

It would be possible to argue that reading the Bible is one of the most important things we ever do.

All-age worship services provide an ideal opportunity to impart both knowledge and understanding of the Bible. Young minds and hearts opened by the Holy Spirit absorb knowledge very quickly, and therefore quite a lot of detail and depth can be covered in one go. It is important to assume no background knowledge, and to explain the context before reading.

God's word is powerful and thrilling. Reading the Bible aloud should be exciting and relevant. It is important to choose a really good reader who is able to give the reading understanding and conviction. Children will soon stop listening if a reader cannot hold their attention. (And let's face it, the adults give up concentrating too. They simply try not to show it!)

The following are a few ideas for reading the Bible in different ways in all-age worship services.

46

Ask a teenager or group of teenagers in advance to put the chosen passage into their own words (using modern language) and to prepare to read out their paraphrase on the day.

47

Select the two or three words that occur most frequently in the Bible passage you have chosen. Write them boldly in advance on separate flash-cards. Choose as many volunteers as you have words and give each of them one of the flash-cards. Each time one of these words occurs in the script, the reader is to pause and indicate to the volunteer with this word to show the flash-card. The congregation then says this single word together, and the reader continues. Good words to choose are 'Lord', the name of the character in the story, or even 'and'.

48

When reading a Bible story prepare a flash-card which says 'and then . . .'. Either choose a volunteer to hold it and show it every time you pause, or show it yourself as often as possible. Everyone calls out 'and then . . .' whenever the flash-card is shown.

49

When reading a Bible story which describes one of the many miracles in the Old or New Testament, prepare flash-

cards with words like 'Wow!', 'Amazing!', 'Can you believe it!' and 'Incredible!'. Other similar words which express surprise or sympathy, such as 'aah' and 'ooh', could be equally appropriate. Choose as many volunteers as you have flash-cards, and prepare them to hold up their words at whatever points you indicate during the reading. Everyone then calls out these expressions as they are displayed.

50

Choose a Bible passage which describes an incident where there would have been lots of noise. The whole congregation is to supply the sound effects. Appropriate sounds should be prepared in advance on flash-cards, and volunteers should be chosen to hold them up for everyone to see whenever you indicate, at the right point in the story. For example, when reading the story of David and Goliath, words such as 'scornful laughter', 'clunk, clunk', 'bubbling water', 'whizz', 'aargh', 'thud' and 'hurray' would be suitable. Or, when reading the story of Jesus and Zacchaeus, words such as 'clinking money', 'running feet', 'swishing branches', 'door shuts', 'angry crowd' and 'loud cheers' would be suitable.

51

People who are not familiar with the Bible often have many mistaken preconceived ideas. They may have no concept of the Bible's remarkable age, historicity, authenticity and preservation. Commonly, the Bible is perceived as a religious book which bears no resemblance to reality and has little relevance today. Alternatively, it may be regarded as a book of legends which is believed by foolish bigots and read only by scholars. Informing the congregation of some little-understood historical facts has the effect of challenging these preconceptions, or, in the case of children, of preventing the preconceptions from gaining a foothold.

Intersperse the reading you have chosen with interesting information about the writer or about the Bible itself. For example, begin the first few verses and then pause and say that hundreds of old manuscripts of the Bible exist. They have been found in different places, and are now in museums around the world. Amazingly, hardly any discrepancies between all the various manuscripts have been found. Although the originals have been lost, this uniformity can only be explained by the existence of a single common original. Manuscripts were carefully copied and stored.

Or, halfway through, interrupt yourself and say something like: 'Do you know how old this book is? It was written nearly 2,000 years ago, and we can read it today!' or, 'Did you know that the Bible is the world's bestselling book of all time? I'm not surprised – it's a must!' If reading from the Gospels, for instance, during the reading say something like: 'Just imagine, John was actually there when all this happened. He watched everything Jesus did, and we can read his very words.' Or, during a reading of one of David's psalms, say something like: 'David wrote this 3,000 years ago and we can read it today!' You get the idea!

52

When reading a non-story passage, such as parts of Paul's epistles or parts of Hebrews or the prophets, first describe its historical context. Then prepare everyone to listen by asking them to imagine that they were the original listeners. For example, ask some to imagine that they are Jews who know only the Old Testament. Ask others to imagine that they are Gentiles who have never heard about Jesus before. Others could imagine themselves as slaves, beggars, murderers or thieves, in prison for their faith or in fear of being persecuted. Find out after the reading how the different groups found it relevant.

53

When reading a story with direct speech, use different voices for the various characters and put on a different hat, scarf or other easily changed accessory as each one speaks. This is easy to do and gives a humorous touch.

54

Single Bible verses can be learned by everyone together during a service using the method described below. As an example, I have chosen Psalm 147:5: 'Great is our Lord and mighty in power; his understanding has no limit.'

First divide the verse into six or so words or phrases, for example: Great is our Lord/and/mighty in power/his understanding/has no limit/Psalm 147:5. Then choose a simple different action to accompany each one of these words or phrases. The actions then become memory aids. For example, start by tapping the top of your head with the palm of your hand. As you do this, say: 'Psalm 147 verse 5.' Then, just tap your head. Everyone should have learned the reference already. Next, introduce the second phrase and its corresponding action. Point upwards with both arms and say, 'Great is our Lord.' Recap by tapping your head and then pointing upwards. The reference and 'great is our Lord' should now have been learned. Practise this once or twice before introducing the third phrase, 'and'. Link the little fingers of both your hands and say, 'And.' Repeat these three simple actions as the congregation repeats together what they have learned so far. An appropriate action to accompany the fourth phrase, 'mighty in power', could be to flex your arm muscles. Again, recap after introducing this. Then introduce the fifth phrase and action. Point to your mind and say, 'His understanding.' Lastly, draw a large imaginary circle to depict the sixth phrase, 'has no limit'. Recap by performing each of the actions randomly to check that each section of the verse has been learned. Then ask the congregation, or individual volunteers, to say the whole verse as you perform the actions. It will have been learned perfectly in no time.

I have deliberately chosen this very easy example to make sure you get the idea. Choosing a longer and more complicated verse to learn in this way is more fun. The same method could be used to teach longer passages of Scripture over several weeks.

Bible Story Dramas

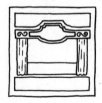

Many Bible stories lend themselves to being read or told using the impromptu participation of everyone present. A drama can be created using the Bible story as the plot and the whole congregation as the cast. Everyone is involved in some way, from the youngest to the oldest – there are no spectators. Teaching the Bible using this method is great fun and very effective. The props and visual aids required are minimal, as the people themselves become the actors, the scenery or the props as necessary!

The entire space you are in becomes the 'stage', be it a tent, a hall, a room or a church. Items of furniture can become props or backdrops as needed – pews can be used to great effect with a little imagination. As there is no audience, elaborate stage equipment like lighting and curtains is not required.

People who are known to enjoy being in the limelight should be chosen to take any central parts. Those who are less extrovert should be included in crowd scenes.

Preparation is required by the director or producer, but no one else. Rehearsals are not necessary. Surprise is an essential element. The idea is not to produce a polished performance, but to involve everybody, have fun and teach the Bible message.

Some simple items of equipment are occasionally required. These are itemised, but are intended to spark your own imagination rather than be rigidly followed.

The text of the Bible itself becomes the basis for any words or speech to be used in the following dramas. There are several ways in which this can happen. Choose which is most appropriate in your situation:

- A summarised version of the Bible text can be put into your own words in advance, and then read aloud on the day.
- The Bible text itself can be read, either as it stands or condensed by omitting sections which are not central to the plot.
- The Bible story can be told ad lib as you go along if you are a good story-teller and are familiar with the text.

When there is a need for the characters to speak, either speak for them using reported speech, e.g. 'And then Moses said . . .', or tell them what to say and when as the story unfolds, or use flash-cards for the actors to read.

55

The people of Israel cross the Red Sea

Bible reference
Exodus 14

Teaching point
Choose from:

(a) God delivers his people from slavery to freedom.
(b) In order to stretch our faith, God sometimes leaves it
      until the last minute before he acts.
(c) Our God is a God of signs and wonders.

Props needed
A bamboo cane to represent Moses' staff.
A tea-towel and rope to become a typical middle-eastern
   head-dress for Moses to wear.

You are to be both the narrator and Moses.
   Put on your head-dress and take your staff as you set the
scene. Explain how God's people had been slaves in Egypt
and how God had chosen Moses to lead them into a new
country which he had promised to give them. When they
left Egypt the King of Egypt followed them, intending to
recapture them. The people of Israel were in a dilemma.
Explain that together you are going to act out what followed.
   Divide the congregation into three. One third is to be the
Red Sea itself, one third will play the part of the people of

Israel, and the final third will be the Egyptian army.

First, ask all those who are to be the Red Sea to assemble themselves. Arrange for them to stand in two long lines. The lines are to face each other, and each person is to hold hands with the person opposite them.

Next, ask those who are to be the people of Israel to bunch together in a large space in a higgledy-piggledy group.

Finally, ask the Egyptian army to stand up where they are, facing the people of Israel and pointing at them.

Instruct the people of Israel to start to show signs of panic as they can see the Egyptians are chasing them. Suggest they call out things like 'Help!' and 'Oh no!'. Instruct them to start shuffling towards one end of the Red Sea.

Instruct the Egyptian army to assemble together and move towards them.

Next ask the Israelites to scream in terror as they arrive at the sea.

Ask the people who are sea to move their arms up and down as though making waves.

Then, Moses is to hold his stick up and over the sea.

At this, those who are the sea start to make the noise of a great wind. They are to lift up their arms above their heads, and thus open a path between the two lines.

The people of Israel then start to walk in single file through the sea to the other side.

Instruct the Egyptian army to follow the people of Israel and start to walk through the sea themselves. Once the people of Israel have all walked through, those playing the part of the sea are to lower their arms again as though the walls of water are collapsing. The Egyptian army then pretends to drown in the water.

Instruct the people of Israel, now all on the other side of the Red Sea, to shout 'Hooray!' and 'Praise God!' in very loud voices.

Once everyone has returned to their seats, make your teaching point.

56

The tabernacle in the wilderness

Bible reference
Exodus 37–40

Teaching point
Choose from:

(a) God wants to live among his people (Exod 25:8).
(b) The meticulous ways which God prescribed for people to approach him in the Old Testament were pictures of Jesus.

Props needed
None.

The aim of this drama is to create a large-scale model of the tabernacle using only people. You will need enough chair-free space to site the 'model'.

Choose four volunteers to sit cross-legged facing each other in a square. They are to hold hands. They represent the brazen altar.

Next, ask two volunteers to stand facing each other, holding hands loosely. These people become the wash-basin or laver.

Then, ask eight people to stand in a straight line. They are to represent the curtain that stood between the outer court and the Holy Place.

On the other side of the curtain, in the Holy Place, was a table and a lampstand. Ask two volunteers to kneel side by side on all fours, so that their backs become the table. Ask five volunteers to be the lampstand. They are to stand in a line, holding hands and holding their arms up. The two people on the ends of the line are to hold up their free arms. Including the middle person's head, the arms thus create seven branches.

One other item of furniture was in the Holy Place, a golden altar. Ask four volunteers to sit cross-legged in a square, facing each other and holding hands, as for the brazen altar.

Choose another eight people to stand in a straight line and so represent the curtain which was between the Holy Place and the Holy of Holies.

Inside the Holy of Holies was the Ark of the Covenant. Ask for a volunteer to kneel on all fours with their head tucked in. Arrange two others on either side, kneeling up and facing each other with their arms above their heads, to reach over the ark. These then represent the cherubim.

A Bible and some communion bread can be placed inside the ark (underneath the person kneeling on all fours), if required. The purpose of these would be to represent the Ten Commandments and the manna which were kept permanently inside the ark.

Finally, ask everyone else to stand in the shape of a rect-angle around the outside, linking arms if possible.

Once everyone is in place describe how the High Priest entered the tabernacle once each year, and made his way past each item of furniture into the Holy of Holies to receive from God forgiveness on behalf of everyone else.

Explain how the inner curtain was torn when Jesus died (Mt 27:51).

57

The twelve spies explore the land of Canaan

Bible reference
Numbers 13

Teaching point
Choose from:

(a) The majority is not always in the right.
(b) Circumstances are always against us to some degree or other. We are overcomers by faith in God.
(c) God will fulfil his promises, however unlikely it might seem.

Props needed
The names of the spies listed in Numbers 13:4–15 written on twelve small pieces of paper.
Hats, dark glasses, scarves, overcoats, etc, to give to the spies to wear in order to make them look incognito.
Drawings or pictures of:
  jars of honey
  corn

bottles of milk
bunches of grapes
pomegranates and figs.
A few short rolls of paper (the back of wallpaper is ideal)
    with bricks drawn on them here and there to look like
    brick walls. (These are for three people standing close
    together to hold around their collective waists and thus
    represent fortified cities.)
A bamboo cane to represent Moses' staff.
A tea-towel and rope to become a typical middle-eastern
    head-dress for Moses to wear.
A sheet of paper with 'There are giants there and the cities
    are fortified' written clearly on one side, and 'God is with
    us – we can surely take the land' written clearly on the
    other. (The spies read these words when they are ques-
    tioned by Moses.)

You are to be both the narrator and Moses.
    Put on your head-dress and take your staff as you set the
scene. Briefly describe the history of the people of Israel,
and how they have now come to the borders of their

promised land. Explain how together everyone will act out the next part of the story.

Ask for twelve volunteers to be the spies. Stand them in a straight line in front of the congregation.

Give each one of the twelve names.

The rest of the congregation is to take the part of the land of Canaan. Ask a volunteer to distribute among the Canaanites who live in Canaan the pictures of the honey, the milk, the corn, the grapes, and the pomegranates and figs, which were plentiful there.

Choose as many sets of three people in the congregation as you have 'walls' to stand up together, holding the walls around themselves and so becoming fortified cities.

Choose a few people to stand on their chairs and so represent some of the giants who lived in Canaan.

Give out an item of the clothing to each spy to wear and so disguise themselves.

Then instruct the twelve spies to walk among the congregation, pretending to explore Canaan.

As they walk in and through the congregation, they are to collect a picture of milk, honey, grapes, corn, pomegranates or figs as they go.

After a short time, ask the spies to reassemble in their straight line at the front, bringing with them their goodies in their hands.

Ask each spy in turn by name what they discovered. Notice the milk, honey, etc. Ask each spy to read out the sentence, 'There are giants there and the cities are fortified.' Joshua and Caleb, of course, are to read out the sentence written on the other side.

Conclude by summing up the outcome of this sad story – the people of Israel wandered in the wilderness for

forty years. Make whichever teaching point you have
chosen.

58

Aaron's budding rod

Bible reference
Numbers 17

Teaching point
Choose from:

(a) God is sovereign and chooses whoever he thinks is best
for particular tasks.
(b) Jesus was God's choice and he alone is our great High
Priest (Heb 7:21). As the dead rod budded, so Jesus rose
from the dead.
(c) God has decided the way we are to approach him. He
has chosen Jesus. Other religions do not lead to God.

Props needed
Thirteen tall bamboo garden canes. Twelve of these are to
be labelled in advance with the names of the twelve tribes
of Israel: Reuben, Simeon, Judah, Issachar, Benjamin,
Ephraim and Manasseh, Zebulun, Dan, Asher, Naphtali,
Gad and Levi. The labels should be fixed to the tops of
the canes. Prepare the thirteenth cane by attaching paper
leaves, almonds and pink flowers down its length with
Sellotape. Hide this cane out of sight.
A tea-towel and rope for a typical middle-eastern head-
dress.

You are to be both the narrator and producer.

Set the scene by explaining how the people of Israel had left Egypt and were on their way to their promised land of Canaan. They were always grumbling about something – usually Moses and Aaron. God grew very angry with their attitude, and decided to show them who was who!

Choose two volunteers to be Moses and Aaron. Give Moses the head-dress to wear.

The congregation are to play the part of the people of Israel. Ask them to complain about Moses and Aaron. Encourage them to shake their fists, and call out things like, 'We've had enough of you, Moses!' or, 'Why should you be our leaders?'

Choose eleven volunteers to stand alongside Aaron and, with him, represent each of the twelve tribes of Israel. Give Aaron the cane which is marked 'Levi', and the other eleven should each have one of the other named canes to hold. Ask Aaron and the eleven volunteers to call out the name of their particular tribe (which is written on their cane).

Next, ask each of the volunteers to lay their cane upright against a suitable wall and behind a suitable curtain. The important thing is to make sure that the labels at the tops of the canes are out of sight.

Night then falls. Ask all the volunteers to return to their seats. Instruct everyone to close their eyes and pretend to sleep. (Ask them to turn and face the other way if you do not trust them to keep their eyes closed for the next few seconds!)

While no one is looking (hopefully!), quickly exchange the cane marked 'Levi' with the prepared thirteenth cane.

Ask the volunteers to line up once more and one by one tell you the name of the tribe they represent. As each one tells you the name of their tribe, select the appropriate cane and return it to them. Make sure that Aaron is the last person to name his tribe.

Reveal Aaron's rod when he calls his name 'Levi'. God had chosen who was to be his high priest.

Ask the volunteers to return to their seats, except Moses and Aaron. Make the teaching point you have chosen.

59

The bronze serpent in the wilderness

Bible reference
Numbers 21:4–9

Teaching point
Choose from:

(a) God hates grumbling.
(b) We are all infected with the selfishness and sin bug. It can be likened to being bitten by a snake; we will die for our sins unless we ask Jesus to forgive us.
(c) Just as the people of Israel looked at the serpent and were saved from death, so we look in faith to Jesus and receive eternal life (Jn 3:14).

Props needed
A vacuum-cleaner hose with a snake's head and forked tongue (cut out of cardboard) attached at one end. Wind this snake around a microphone stand, and position it outside in another room, hidden from the congregation.
A bamboo cane to represent Moses' staff.
A tea-towel and rope to become a typical middle-eastern head-dress for Moses.

You are the narrator. First, set the scene. The people of Israel were wandering in the wilderness, having failed to enter their

promised land. They hated it, even though God was very
good to them.

Choose someone to play the part of Moses. Dress them
in the head-dress and give them the staff.

Choose a few people who are to play the parts of the serpents.

The rest of the congregation are to pretend to be the
people of Israel.

Ask the congregation to start grumbling and complaining to one another. Suggest they say loudly things like:
'We're fed up with this place'; 'When are we ever going to
get somewhere?'; 'It's so hot in this wilderness.'

Instruct the serpents to move among the congregation
and lightly pinch one or two people each. The people who
have been 'bitten' are then to pretend that they have
become very sick.

At this, the people of Israel become very frightened.
They stop complaining and start to say sorry for their attitude problem. Encourage them to adopt prayerful positions as if asking God for forgiveness.

Instruct Moses to pretend to pray for the people and ask
God to show him what to do.

Then ask Moses to instruct the people who have been
bitten, and who are continuing to be very sick, to walk to
the place where the model of the serpent on the pole is
situated. Once there, they are to take a good look at the
image, where they are healed. Then they are to return to
their seats.

While this is happening, the serpents continue to bite the
rest of the congregation until everyone has had a chance to
go and look at the serpent on the pole.

Finish by making your teaching point.

60

Joshua and the people of Israel take Jericho

Bible reference
Joshua 6

Teaching point
Choose from:

(a) God can change impossible circumstances.
(b) God wants his people to make progress in their
     Christian lives. Sometimes there are large obstacles he
     wants us to face and tackle.

Props needed
Seven 'trumpets' for the priests – long cardboard tubes
    covered with coloured paper, or seven cheap party
    hooters.
A cardboard box covered in gold paper, or two plain hori-
    zontal wooden chairs with their legs interlocked, to
    represent the ark.
A length of red ribbon to hang from Rahab's house.

You are to be both the narrator and Joshua.
    Set the scene by explaining how all the older generation,
including Moses, had died. Now is the time when at last
the people of Israel are ready to enter their promised land,
Canaan. The people who lived in Canaan were extremely
wicked, and God had told the people of Israel to destroy
them. The first city to be conquered was Jericho.

Choose seven volunteers to be priests. Give each of them a trumpet. They are to be the leaders of the march around the city walls.

Next, choose a few people to be a small armed guard. Perhaps you could choose people who have been in the forces or cadets. Instruct half of them to assemble themselves behind the priests.

Next, choose two volunteers to carry the ark. They too are to join the march, followed by the rest of the armed guard.

Finally, ask all the children present to line up behind.

Those who are left in the congregation are to pretend they are the city of Jericho. Instruct the people sitting around the edges to stand up and so become the walls.

Give one person who is standing in the wall the red ribbon to hold. This person is to play the part of Rahab.

The marching can now begin. The priests are to lead, blowing their trumpets. The whole procession is to circle Jericho once.

This procession is to be repeated five more times, and then seven more times. If circling this many times would be too time consuming, simply explain how Joshua, the people and the ark circled the city every day for one week, and finally walked round seven times at once.

During the last circuit, order everyone who is marching to make lots of noise.

At the tremendous sound, those standing as the walls are to collapse and fall over. Only the person holding the ribbon is to stay upright.

Instruct the people who are part of the procession to walk through the walls into Jericho, and thus return to their seats. They have taken the city.

Finish by making your teaching point.

61

Gideon and his army defeat the Midianites

Bible reference
Judges 7:15–22

Teaching point
Choose from:

(a) God fills ordinary repentant people with his Holy Spirit and uses them (Judg 6:25–34).
(b) God helps us to overcome long-standing problems (enemies).
(c) God has a different strategy for each situation.
(d) Numbers are not important. Jesus said in Luke 12:32, 'Do not be afraid, little flock, for your Father has been pleased to give you the kingdom.'

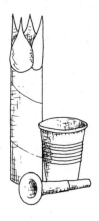

Props needed

Kitchen roll-sized cardboard tubes with one end painted
   red to represent torches.

Party hooters to represent trumpets.

Plastic cups to represent pitchers or jars.

You are to be both the narrator and Gideon.

Set the scene by describing how the people of Israel had
been disobeying God by worshipping false gods, and the
Midianite armies were marauding them. They had prayed
to God for help, and God had visited Gideon and chosen
him to lead the army which would defeat the Midianites.
His army was very small.

Choose a number of children to be in your army.
Everyone else is to play the parts of the Midianites.

Give each member of your army a torch, a pitcher and a
trumpet. The plastic cups are to be placed over the red ends
of the torches.

Position your army around the outside of the seated
Midianites. Each soldier is to stand one by one at regular
intervals around the circumference.

When they are in position, give the army their instructions. First, everyone is to blow their trumpets. Next,
they are to stamp on their plastic cups and crush
them. Finally, they are to hold up their torches and
shout loudly together, 'The sword of the Lord and of
Gideon.'

At this point, all those who are Midianites scream in
terror and kill each other!

At the end, make the teaching point.

62

Jonah

Bible reference
Jonah 1–4

Teaching point
Choose from:

(a) God loves people who do not acknowledge him.
(b) God is grieved by wickedness and 'commands all people everywhere to repent' (Acts 17:30).
(c) God is merciful. The Assyrians were a cruel and violent people who did not acknowledge him.
(d) We can get really fed up and angry when we are personally inconvenienced, and fail to see the more important issues.

Section one: God calls Jonah

Props needed
A tea-towel with a rope to make a typical middle-eastern head-dress.

You are the narrator.
   Ask for a volunteer to play the part of Jonah. Put on the head-dress.
   Set the scene. Explain how God had spoken to Jonah and told him that he must travel to Nineveh, the Assyrian capital city, and then preach to the people who lived there.

Instruct Jonah to run around the outside of the congregation to represent him running away from God.

Ask sixteen or so people in a middle section of the congregation to play the parts of the sailors and the boat. Eight of them are to pretend to be sailors and the other eight people surrounding them are to become the boat itself. Ask them to stand.

Choose a person sitting near to the boat to become the captain.

Ask Jonah to pay his fare to the captain and then squeeze into the boat with the sailors. He is then to fall asleep.

Now ask the rest of the congregation to pretend they are the sea. Instruct them to make a noise like the wind blowing and to wave their arms up and down and stand up and then sit down, thus representing a storm. Give them an opportunity to experiment with some Mexican waves for huge breakers.

While they are doing this, instruct the people playing the part of the boat to make creaking sounds. At this point, the sailors are to call out in terror to their gods.

Then instruct the sailors to pretend to throw cargo overboard in panic.

Ask the captain to wake up Jonah who has been asleep all this time.

Explain how Jonah told his story to the sailors.

Instruct the sailors to start rowing, while the storm continues. After a short while the sailors are to have a discussion. Finally, they agree that they will throw Jonah overboard.

Next, choose eight or so people in the congregation sitting near to the boat to play the part of the great fish. Instruct the sailors to pick up Jonah and throw him into the sea. Those who are now playing the part of the fish are to catch him. As soon as Jonah is in the fish, the sea calms down.

Instruct the sailors to adopt prayerful positions as though they are asking God for forgiveness and acknowledging his greatness.

Section two: Inside the fish

Props needed
None.

Jonah is in the fish and cries out to God. Choose some suitable verses from Jonah 2 to read out.

Then instruct the people who are the fish to cross their hands together to make a seat for Jonah. They are then to carry him out of the sea and deposit him on dry land.

Section three: Jonah goes to Nineveh

Props needed
A cardboard crown and simple robe for the king.
A stool for the king to sit on.
A dustbin liner with holes cut out for the head and arms for the king to wear when he repents.

Ask for a volunteer to play the part of the King of Assyria. He is to sit on the stool and wear the robe and crown.

The rest of the congregation now pretend they are the people of Nineveh.

Ask Jonah to walk around the circumference of the congregation, as though he were walking from the beach where the fish deposited him to Nineveh.

Next, instruct Jonah to walk in and out of the congrega-

tion. As he does so he is to call out: 'Forty more days and
Nineveh will be overturned.'

Instruct each member of the congregation to kneel as
Jonah passes by, acting as though they were asking God for
forgiveness for their sins.

While this is happening, the king is to take off his crown
and robe, pull the dustbin liner over his head and sit down
on the ground with his head in his hands.

Once Jonah has finished and everyone is kneeling,
instruct the king to declare a public fast and lead his people
in a prayer of repentance.

Section four: Jonah is fed up

Props needed
A six-foot length of rope which has large paper leaves
    attached down its length at various intervals with
    Sellotape. Coil the rope into a plastic carrier bag. (This is
    to be the plant.)
A chair for Jonah to sit by.
A large picture or drawing of a burning sun.

Choose a volunteer to be ready to hold the sun up when
needed.

Place the carrier bag with 'the plant' hidden in it behind
the chair.

Instruct Jonah to sit by the chair and pretend to be in a
very angry mood.

Next, put your hand in the carrier bag and, taking one end
of the rope, step up onto the chair, slowly pulling 'the plant'
out of the bag. Hold it up to its full length above Jonah.

With the congregation, count from one to forty (to
indicate the passing days). After forty, lead the congrega-

tion in a cheer to celebrate their escape from destruction. As the cheering goes on, Jonah is to pretend he is more miserable than ever.

Instruct the volunteer with the sun to hold it above Jonah's head.

Then lower the plant slowly to the ground to represent it withering and dying.

Instruct Jonah to get up and stamp his foot, as though he were really angry with God.

Jonah is concerned about himself and his comforts. God loved the world so much that he gave his only Son . . . (Jn 3:16). Make your teaching point.

63

The parable of the great feast

Bible reference
Luke 14:15–24

Teaching point
Choose from:

(a) God has a special love for those who are poor, disabled or socially unaccepted.
(b) God's invitation of mercy goes out to all people without exception.
(c) When God calls us it is important not to make excuses.
(d) There is going to be a wonderful celebration when Jesus returns.

Props needed
None.

This drama needs enough furniture-free space to enable everyone present to assemble in a group.

You are the narrator and the man who gives the feast.

Choose two or three volunteers to be your servants.

Choose several people to play the parts of those who refuse their invitations. Ask them to stand.

Instruct the servants to go to each of the people who are standing and give them an invitation to the forthcoming banquet. These people are to make excuses, and then sit down.

Next ask everyone present to hide themselves somewhere – under pews or chairs, behind curtains, behind furniture, under mats, etc. No one should be left sitting in their seat.

Instruct the servants to go out into the 'streets and alleys of the town' and invite everyone they find to the great feast. The servants are then to look for those who are in hiding, and on finding someone they are to accompany them to the open space.

As the servants return with a guest, send them off again to search for someone else, until everyone has been found and has assembled for the feast.

Once everyone has gathered, explain how merciful God is, and how he invites not the great and the good, but the ordinary and the bad to his feast! Make your teaching point.

Play some music and start the dancing! A song, such as 'The Feast' or 'He brought me to his banqueting table', could be sung together to finish.

Raps

The following raps were not difficult to write. The Bible is full of good stories, and the range covered here is of necessity severely limited. Raps are great fun, and they can serve the purpose of teaching or recapping Bible stories. They can be used in almost any context.

When using raps in public, choose good, clear readers who are willing to practise beforehand. The scanning needs to be rehearsed so that the emphasis falls in the right place in each line. The beat needs to be kept going. This means emphasising the beat and having a drum rhythm going at the same time. During the breaks the drums can introduce a new rhythm. Many electric keyboards have drum beats which are ideal for accompanying raps. They can be as sophisticated or as simple as you like. Alternatively, the congregation can all click their fingers in time.

Why not have a go at writing some of your own?

64

There is a curious convolution –
A theory labelled 'evolution'.
It says there was no God involved
But by some fluke we all evolved.
Things look designed, but that's illusion,
Meant to add to our confusion.
The Bible takes a different tack
So sit and listen to this rap.

Back then, right at the start of time,
God spoke these words: 'Let light now shine.'
A watery ball became all bright
Dark oceans beamed with sparkling light.
First the water, then the photon;
History's first page was wrote on.
A brand new world began to spin
Day One passed by, Day Two came in.

God moved the water there and here
And made huge space and atmosphere.
Dry land appeared, uncultivated,
But fertilised and rotivated.
The earth turned on, another spin,
Day Two passed by, Day Three came in.

Next came the plants and forests neat;
The world turned green and looked a treat;
Swamps, bogs and marshes, grass and sedge,
Orchards, flowers, fruit and veg.

The earth turned on, another spin,
Day Three passed by, Day Four came in.

Atomic bombs went off in space
And stars popped up all round the place;
Millions, trillions, it was done
And one small star became our sun.
Man, what a mega innovation –
The universe in syncopation!
The lot span round, Day Four was done;
Day Five had only just begun.

God got up early, spoke the word
And every kind of fish and bird
Filled the rivers, lakes and seas
Hedges, bushes, shrubs and trees.
God said, 'Get cracking, have some fun.
All reproduce, have lots of young.'
The earth turned on, another spin.
Day Five passed by, Day Six came in.

Huge creatures, dinosaurs and whales
And little ones, like ants and snails;
Different shapes and different habits –
Lions, elephants and rabbits –
Designed by God, all were created;
And each pair lost no time and mated.

God saw it all looked pretty neat.
The universe was now complete –
A great big stage which God had set
For his most awesome brainwave yet –
A man called Adam, with Eve, his wife;

God blew in both the breath of life.
Day Six was done. God took a rest.
And all that he had made was blessed –
A perfect whole, quite self-contained;
Now by his mighty power maintained.

Six days sounds fast you might be thinking –
But from his word we have an inkling
That we will one day have new parts,
New eyes and ears, new hands, new hearts.
He'll recreate us while we're blinking
In an instant, in a twinkling.
There will be one celebration,
When God completes his new creation!
God's power's amazing, mega, brill,
It's awesome, vast, immense and skill.

Genesis 1

65

Do you know about the origins of the human race?
Do you know where we came from, how we lost the
    case?
Do you know the story of what happened long ago?
Listen to this rap, and I'll tell you what was so.

The one true God, as I'm sure you understand,
Took some ordinary soil in the palm of his hand.
He formed a man whom he energised with life
And while he slept, from his bone, made him a wife.
One single man plus a female sensation,
Together the pinnacle of God's creation.
Male and female, God's image they reflected
Alive and full of joy, really good, perfected.

'The earth is all yours,' God said, 'to run and own.
Everything is here, it's your great dream home.
There is just one thing you must never ever do –
Do not eat the fruit from this tree I'm showing you.
This is a serious warning, eat and you will die.
You must obey my word; this one law do not defy.'

But Eve was sorely tempted and thought that she could
    eat.
The crafty serpent told her that the fruit was sweet.
He said, 'All knowledge will belong to you;
You'll have power, you'll be wise, and do what God can
    do.'
Eve stretched her hand out and picked a single fruit.

She ate and husband Adam ate to boot.
The fruit was digested; there were awful contortions
And evil consequences of terrible proportions.
They disobeyed, sin was enthroned,
And God's entire creation groaned.
What could they do? They could only run and hide;
Fear was in their hearts and perfect love had died.

'Where are you, Adam?' God called to his friend.
Their Father–son relationship was sadly at an end.
Lost and feeling naked, God covered them with skins,
Promising a Son who would one day cover sins.
From that time on loads of wickedness, ambition
Have filled each heart – it's the human condition.
Sin and madness rule and the world is in a mess,
All of us are guilty, but God has planned to bless.

The mighty Jesus came to forgive man's sin;
And take away the evil which is deep within.
He gave his life up for every single one –
To mend the relationship of Father and son.
Now all across the world every adult, every child
With the great Creator can be reconciled.
You can be safe from destruction that's to come,
A member of his family, hidden in his Son.
He will forgive, no need to share the blame;
He will rescue you, if you call on his name.
Ask him to reverse the effects of the Fall;
Receive his great salvation which is free to all.

Genesis 3

66

He was the first and he made the lot,
He was equal with the Father and he was begot.
Willing to relinquish his heavenly position,
He came to earth to share our human condition.

So Jesus moved down here, an ordinary bloke,
Exactly right on with every word he spoke.
Without a selfish thought and completely free of pride,
He was humble to the finish when he bled and died.

His incarnation is a total mystery –
The biggest downgrade ever seen in history.
Because of his obedience, God has said,
'Jesus to the top, when I raise him from the dead.'

So Jesus is now sitting on the highest throne
No other king is near him, he is quite alone.
He is ruler of the universe and there will be a day
When 'Jesus is Lord' everyone will kneel and say.

So followers of Jesus must be humble too;
Chuck out all our pride and be selfless through and
    through.
We must never chafe, grumble or complain,
For Jesus is our model and we represent his name.

When those around are mean and selfish, ready for a fight,
We obey the one who is the Lord of light.

We shine like stars in a blackened sky –
Witnesses to Jesus till the day we die.

Philippians 2:6–15

67

We've got some news guys, did you know
That one day time will go real slow?
This world will end and fall apart
And everlasting life will start.
A shout will carry all around
And God's loud trumpet blast will sound.
We'll all see Jesus in the sky
And as we see him, we shall fly –
We'll rise, we'll soar up in the air
And meet our Saviour Jesus there.
All those who snuffed it long ago
Will live again and steal the show.
With brand new bodies they will rise
As we all watch with great surprise.
All sin and pain will be no more,
All evil will go out the door.
No sadness, no infirmity,
Just joy for all eternity.
The earth and sky will be repealed
And brand new ones will be revealed.
Hey guys, no need to sit and mope
We have a great, tremendous hope.

1 Thessalonians 4:13–18

68

You are God's own children, Jesus gave his life for you;
So follow his example and be righteous through and through.
Don't be a lazy toad, slum around or sit and lounge;
Work for your own living, never think to steal or scrounge.
Do not get annoyed, keep complaining or be rude;
Do not be a person who develops 'attitude'.
Never swear or curse or use words that are profane;
Never tell crude jokes or make light of Jesus' name.

You are not in darkness, you have stepped into the light.
You should not be dunces, but intelligent and bright.
Don't depend on alcohol or fraternise the boozer,
Contentment will elude you and you'll always be a loser.
To really live it up, here's the line that you must toe –
Ask God for his Spirit till you overflow.
Give lots of thanks, sing out lots of songs of praise;
Don't be shy and timid, but speak out in lots of ways.

Wives, this is a must that God has said to you –
Look up to your husband, disrespect will never do.
Do not boss or nag – this is terrible behaviour;
Submit to your own man and submit to your own Saviour.
Husbands, God says plainly you must love your wives;
When you have a row do not dig in with the knives;
Do not be a chauvinist, full of your concerns;
Investing in your wife produces excellent returns.

Children, always do whatever Mum and Dad require –
For this is cool behaviour that has got to inspire.

Mum and Dad, be patient and give lots of time for play;
Do not rule the roost in an authoritarian way.
At work always be conscientious, go the second mile;
Never once be seen without a cheerful, willing smile.
You've been born again, you are revolutionised;
All your thoughts and actions must be really scrutinised.

The world is full of sin and pain and in a dreadful mess –
Hooking up to Jesus is the life that God will bless.
Obeying his instructions brings abundant life,
Free from lots of pain and anguish, sin and strife.
Live each day by faith – you'll be wearing a shield;
Read up on the Bible – it's a sword to wield.
God's way is like a helmet which you always wear,
Protecting you from evil and from Satan's snare.
Forgiveness, transformation and then final celebration –
We have got the lot with our incredible salvation.

Ephesians 4:29–6:18

69

A VIP was travelling to the town of Jericho.
The news was spreading fast, there wasn't one who didn't
    know –
A blind beggar, Bart, was shouting, 'I can see
Here's the Son of David, who had mercy on me!
Here's the Son of David, who had mercy on me!'

When old Zacchaeus heard the news, he stopped right in
    his tracks –
He was a mean and wealthy guy who liked collecting tax.

He wasn't very popular, you could say he was hated,
The way he robbed and cheated folks was not appreciated.
The way he robbed and cheated folks was not appreciated.

The town was out in numbers, they were lining every
street.
Now Zack was very short, in fact, he barely reached five
feet.
He couldn't see above the heads, the crowd was sixteen
deep –
He would never get a look-in or a peep.
He would never get a look-in or a peep.

'Buzz off,' they said, 'you little shrimp, do you hear what
we say?

Clear off, get lost, go home, because you're getting in our
way.'
Zacchaeus had a brainwave: 'Why don't I climb that tree?
I'll get a real good view from there; this Jesus I must see.
I'll get a real good view from there; this Jesus I must see.'

Zacchaeus ran ahead as he had never run before
And shinned into the branches of a leafy sycamore.
He perched inside the tree and looked out through leaves
    of green.
Now he could see it all, but he himself could not be seen.
Now he could see it all, but he himself could not be seen.

He held his breath when he saw Jesus stop right under-
    neath;
His heart began to beat, he started shaking like a leaf.
Jesus looked him in the eye and said, 'Zack, come on down.
It is for you, my friend, that I have visited this town.
It is for you, my friend, that I have visited this town.'

The crowd were shocked and horrified; they hissed and
    then they booed,
They shook their fists in anger; there was quite an ugly
    mood.
But Jesus was determined, he was not to be deterred;
Compassion burned within him and his heart was being
    stirred.
Compassion burned within him and his heart was being
    stirred.

Privately he said to Zack, 'Now what I say is true,
I have come to seek and save all sinners lost like you.
Zack, it's time to change your ways, from trickery relent,
You must give up stealing and quite thoroughly repent.
You must give up stealing and quite thoroughly repent.'

Zack cried as he listened and he listened as he cried,
His sinful, sneaky, selfish ways he never once denied.
'I'll repay all that I owe, and even times by four;

I'm sorted and I'm saved, and that's worth a whole lot
   more!
I'm sorted and I'm saved, and that's worth a whole lot
   more!'

Luke 19:1–10

70

To Herod's Temple Courts all the Jewish people came
To catch a glimpse of Jesus – he was a famous name.
Jesus was there teaching and the Pharisees and Scribes
Were there to make sure he got all the jip and jibes.
Were there to make sure he got all the jip and jibes.

A woman stood in public for everyone to see,
They said she was committing adultery.
'This woman is a sinner,' the Pharisees declared,
'It was not with her own husband that her bed was being
   shared.
She was having a relationship, living in sin,
We knew you would be here, so we brought her in.
We knew you would be here, so we brought her in.

'Come on, Jesus, surely this is sin you can't condone.
The law of Moses clearly says that she should be stoned.'
Now this was tricky, Jesus needed time to sit and ponder;
He looked down at the ground and then doodled with his
   finger.
Crowds of people gathered round, eyes open wide.
What would Jesus answer? The Pharisees were right.
What would Jesus answer? The Pharisees were right.

Jesus stood and slowly said, 'Now what you say is true.
I've read the books of Moses and I do agree with you.
So anyone here who wants to have a go
And who has never sinned himself can take a stone to
  throw.
And who has never sinned himself can take a stone to
  throw.'

The people were astonished and the Pharisees were
  stunned.
Jesus sat back down again and wrote upon the ground.
The scribes were taken down a peg, quite humiliated;
Such a clever answer they had not anticipated.
Such a clever answer they had not anticipated.

Their tails between their legs, they turned and went back
  home.
Jesus and the woman were left there all alone.
Not one there to point a finger, all had made their choice.
Jesus asked, 'Where are they all?' with sympathetic voice.
The woman said, 'I had my eyes fastened to the ground.
I am so ashamed – I did not mean to sleep around.
I am so ashamed – I did not mean to sleep around.'

'I do not condemn you; I won't be pressing charges;
But now the time has come for you to think about some
  changes.
Go home now,' said Jesus, 'sin no more.
Your sins are all forgiven; you have heaven in store.
Your sins are all forgiven; you have heaven in store.'

God is mega-merciful, he knows we all are sinners;
He knows our evil, selfish ways outnumber our hot dinners.

He's made a way to put us right, to straighten and unbend
   us
He gave his Son to do the deal, forgive us and then mend
   us.
Sin may look tempting, but afterwards we're iller.
Doing right is best for all and guilt is such a killer.
The truth that we're forgiven sets us really free
And gives us power to be the people we were meant to be.
Jesus said, 'I am the light, the life, the truth, the way.'
You'd better believe it, turn around and follow him today.

John 8:1–12

71

Now Jesus, he went right on saying
You should never give up praying.
Suppose one night at 12 o'clock
Right on your door you hear a knock;
Now you turn over straight away
'Cos you have had a real long day.
But then you hear that knock again –
'Oh go away, it's well past ten!'
(This is the time you went to bed
Because you had a splitting head.)
But from his task he don't recoil
That guy downstairs makes your blood boil.
He starts to shout and make a din
'Aw, come on down and let me in;
This mate of mine has just called by
And I don't have not one french fry.
Now he's well-starved and really lean

And it would make me look so mean
If I could not just offer him
Some toast or baked beans from a tin.
Just shake yourself from rest and ease
And slip downstairs to your deep-freeze.
You must have something hidden there
Something tasty you can spare.'
You mumble, 'I thought him my friend;
He must be nuts. This is the end.
He must be crazy to keep knocking.
It makes my head hurt something shocking.'
You must get up, no other way
To get some peace from this affray.
You shove some burgers in his hand
A pizza and some baked beans canned.
You say to him, 'Now you get lost
Before you have to pay the cost
Of my lost sleep and shattered nerve
A big black eye's what you deserve!'
And Jesus said, 'Now listen good
And hear me out, because you should.
Just keep on praying like that guy
Because our Father there on high
Don't sleep or get annoyed with us
When we keep on and make a fuss.
He likes to give us what we need,
And does it quick at double speed.
So check out first what you require
Is good and right, not just desire,
And keep right on that praying task –
God gives to those who ask and ask.'

Luke 11:5–8

72

The Acts of the Apostles tells the story of Saul
Who persecuted Christians 'cos he hated them all.
The church was really growing in all kinds of different places –
Wherever you went there were always new faces.
Saul began to note the names of those who had converted –
It was curtains for them all unless they reverted.
The fact that many synagogues had been infiltrated
And many priests had come to Christ was not appreciated.
He thought that he was doing God a big favour –
A Pharisee was he, of conservative flavour.
A Pharisee was he, of conservative flavour.

There were converts in Damascus now, and Saul was not amused.
He would need to make the trip and see them all accused.
He set off in a fury, with papers duly signed.
Orthodox Jewry was being undermined.
Orthodox Jewry was being undermined.

Breathing out blue murder, he journeyed to the town –
Damascus was in sight when Saul's world turned upside down.
Out of nowhere, suddenly, a bright light shone.
A voice called, 'Saul, you won't like this, but you're wrong.
You are persecuting, not my followers, but me.

This is a serious matter, I am sure you will agree.
This is a serious matter, I am sure you will agree.'

Saul was a worried man, he was quivering in his boots.
If I am not mistaken he was shaken to the roots.
'Who are you, Lord?' he in fear and trembling said.
'I am Jesus, King of kings and risen from the dead.
I am Jesus, King of kings and risen from the dead.'

'Go into Damascus, to the street called Straight.
When you arrive you must sit and wait.
I will tell you what to do. I have chosen you
To preach to the Gentile as well as the Jew.
To preach to the Gentile as well as the Jew.'

Saul couldn't see a thing and he was really scared.
For such a confrontation he was rather unprepared.
His friends helped him to his feet and led him by the
    hand.
There was lots of stuff he just couldn't understand.
There was lots of stuff he just couldn't understand.

He did not eat a single thing but fasted for three days,
In desperate repentance for his murderous ways.
Could it be that Christians were right all along?
Could it be that it was he who'd got it all wrong?
If Jesus was the Christ, not some error or a fake –
How could he have made such a terrible mistake?
How could he have made such a terrible mistake?

When Ananias came and prayed, his eyes became OK.
Filled with the Spirit he was baptised the same day.
In a single U-turn, no attempt to save his face,

He asked for forgiveness from the God of grace.
He changed completely, no longer was he Saul.
Sold out for Jesus was the new man Paul.
Sold out for Jesus was the new man Paul.

Acts 9:1–18

Testimonies

Testimonies provide an excellent means of communicating the fact that the whole of life belongs to God, and that Christianity has nothing to do with religion and everything to do with a living relationship with Jesus Christ.

Testimonies should be concise, factual and natural, with no hint of professionalism or 'churchy language'. Preparation beforehand is essential. Those who are not used to speaking in public should write out a testimony in advance and then read it on the day. Doing this does not inhibit spontaneity and has several advantages: it calms nerves and avoids stage-fright; it keeps the speaker concise and to the point; and it tells everyone that the person has thought carefully about what they want to say.

The following ideas may help you to think of some different ways of including testimony in all-age worship services.

73

Ask someone to think about how they became a Christian. Give them the following questions to answer: Where? When? Why? How? What happened at the time and afterwards?

74

Ask two friends to talk about how God has blessed them through one another.

75

Ask someone to think of an incident in their lives which was very significant to them. How do they relate the incident to their Christian faith?

76

Ask someone who has recently become a Christian to describe how they used to see God, and how they see him now. What did they used to think about Jesus? What do they think about him now? What did they used to think about church? What do they think about it now?

77

Ask someone to describe briefly a typical day in their life, explaining how God is real to them in their ordinary routine.

78

Ask some children to summarise what they have been learning about in Sunday school and how what they have learned has been important in their daily lives.

79

Ask someone to describe their experience of the Holy Spirit, how he fills them, how he is real to them in their Christian lives. What changes in themselves have they become aware of?

80

Read a psalm, such as Psalm 34, or selected verses from the Psalms, and as you read, ask people to stand or put up their hands if they have personally experienced the truth of a particular verse. If desired, ask one or two people to explain briefly what happened and how the sentiments of the verse became reality in their lives.

81

In advance ask a parent and child to prepare a list of things
that they have learned from each other and then ask them
to talk about them briefly.

82

In advance ask an older person to prepare a list of things
which they have come to realise are the most important
things in life. Then ask them to talk briefly about them.

Quizzes

Quizzes are a very useful tool to use in all-age worship services. All ages enjoy them, and they offer an opportunity for shyer people to participate. They are an ideal boredom stopper for children. Also, perhaps most important of all, they offer a fun opportunity to recap on information which you want everyone to remember.

There are endless ways of creating teams so that everyone is involved. They can be teams of boys versus girls, or young versus old, or people sitting to the left versus those to the right, etc. A quiz between children and adults is really enjoyed by the children. In this case make sure that the adults are given difficult questions!

Quizzes should not go on for too long. Twelve questions in all is plenty, and the questions should be carefully chosen so that anyone who has been present and listening can answer. A quiz should not give an opportunity for those with Mensa-level IQs or long years of Bible knowledge to show off. A newcomer should be able to answer as well as an old-timer. The aim of a quiz is not to play a game of Trivial Pursuit, but to provide an opportunity for revision and reinforcement following a talk, a Bible reading or a drama. Careful listening is encouraged if you warn everyone that a quiz will follow.

Fun can be had if quizzes include an element of chance in the scoring. Then the outcome is not easily predictable. (I have found Children Worldwide have excellent resources, including many quizzes. For one of their mail order catalogues write to: Children Worldwide, Dalesdown, Honeybridge Lane, Dial Post, Horsham, West Sussex RH13 8NX Tel: 01403 710712.)

83

Prepare an overhead projector slide with sixteen squares. Number the squares with the numbers minus one, nought, one and two, so that each number occurs four times randomly.

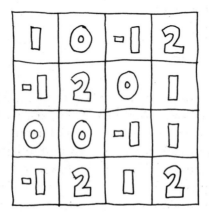

When a team member answers a question correctly, a representative of the team drops a tiddlywink onto the acetate from about 20cms. Everyone will be able to see where the tiddlywink comes to rest. If it falls on a line, the lower score counts.

A scoring system will be needed. One of the simplest and most fun ways of counting the score is to use a line of people for each team. One person in the line stands for one point. People are added to the line as points are scored. If a minus point is scored, someone returns to their seat.

84

Have some answers in a hat. Use names of characters or places, such as 'Darius', 'Daniel' or 'Babylon'. One team member draws out one of the answers and members of the other team are to pose as many questions as they can think of that would fit it. The winning team is the team that suggests the most questions.

85

Have four questions written on pieces of paper and folded separately in one box, and the four answers folded separately in another. A team member, without looking, selects a question randomly, and then, also without looking, selects an answer from the box of answers. If the two fit, points are scored and the question and answer removed. If they don't fit together, both the question and the wrong answer are replaced in their boxes. The teams continue to take turns until all the questions are paired with their answers.

86

Prepare eleven identical pieces of A5-size card. Prepare five large dots of one colour and six similar dots in a second contrasting colour. Stick the dots onto the backs of the eleven cards and lay them randomly, dot-side down, on a table top. The colour of the dots underneath each card should not be visible.

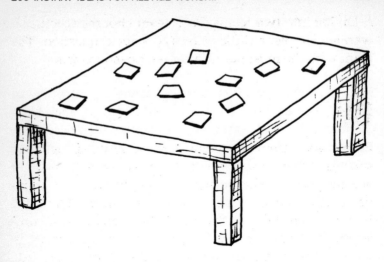

Prepare eleven questions. Each time a team member answers a question correctly, they pick up one of the cards without looking underneath. Having chosen one, the team member holds up their card so that the colour of the dot is visible to everyone.

The first team to collect four dots of the same colour wins.

87

Prepare five simple questions, five more difficult questions and five 'pot luck' questions and put them in different boxes. Mark each of the 'pot luck' questions with either minus one, nought, one, two or three points. A difficult question will always score two points, and a simple one one point.

Divide into two teams. Each team chooses whether it wants a simple, a difficult or a 'pot luck' question. The team with the most points after ten questions wins.

88

Divide volunteers into teams of three. Write out as many shortish Bible verses as you have teams on a piece of acetate and cut the verses into single words. Choose verses that no one would know by heart. Place the words of one of the verses randomly on an overhead projector. One team is to try to arrange the words into a sentence. Time them, and repeat for the other teams. The winning team is the one which sorts out a sentence in the shortest time.

89

Put up a dart board in a safe place and for safety reasons have just one dart available. When a team answers a question correctly, a member of the team is to throw the dart at the board. They score whatever number they hit on the board. If the dart falls out after two attempts, the score is zero.

90

Have a dice and shaker available. When a team answers a question correctly, a member of the team shakes the dice. They score whatever number is shown on the dice.

91

Divide everyone into small groups and give each group a pen and lots of paper. Also give each group a copy of the same enlarged photocopied Bible portion, chosen to fit the theme. Have ready ten key words chosen from this portion.

Ask a representative from each group to come forward. Show them the first key word on your list, keeping the others hidden. The representatives then return to their own groups and draw clues to enable the other members of the group to guess what it is. No words must be spoken and no verse numbers used as hints. Once the first word has been guessed, another member of the group tells you the answer and then returns to their group to draw the second word. This continues until all ten words have been guessed. The first group to finish is the winner.

Response

God has given his Son Jesus Christ to the world, and he is looking for a response. God is active, always speaking and working, always engaging in the affairs of men, calling individuals to a relationship with himself. Ignoring him is not the best option!

Responsiveness to God is to be encouraged from an early age, in the little things of life as well as the big things. Here are some ideas which you can use during all-age services to encourage response.

92

Jesus says that his followers can be described as jewels in his crown (Zech 9:16). Each member of the congregation is to be represented by a jewel stuck onto a large crown.

In advance make a crown out of white tissue paper. Use one rectangular sheet and cut out four equal triangles

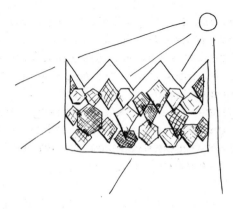

along one long edge to make the shape of a crown. Stiffen the perimeter by edging it with black insulating tape. (Do this on a flat surface, as the tissue tears easily, but it is not as difficult as it sounds.) On the day, attach it to a suitable window with Blutack.

Have scissors, Pritt sticks and lots of small pieces of tissue paper in different colours on a table nearby. During the singing of a song, ask people to come to this table in twos or threes and cut a small jewel shape out of the tissue paper to represent themselves. Next, each one is invited to stick the 'jewel' onto the white crown background. Overlapping does not matter.

Alternatively, for speed, have plenty of diamond- or heart-shaped pieces of tissue paper in different colours ready-made. Ask each person present to choose a shape and stick it onto the crown.

93

Everyone present who wants to be included in the church which Jesus said he would build (Mt 16:18) is to be involved in creating a human body shape by sitting close together to form the shape on the floor.

This response requires enough space for everyone present to assemble together and sit closely compacted on the floor. Choose a group of people to form the shape of a head by packing together (two people wearing blue can be the eyes and four wearing red can be the lips, etc.). Choose another group and ask them to sit together in the shape of a neck and trunk. Two further groups are to form themselves into the shapes of arms and hands, and two final groups are to assemble together in the shape of legs and feet. Leave each group to organise themselves and then to link up their parts to the whole body. Each group is to sit down on the floor once they are in position. Someone might like to stand on a chair or stepladder to take an 'aerial photograph' once everyone is ready.

If numbers are too few for the body shape to be filled with people, ask people to create the body outline, using the same method.

Everyone can be part of the church. There is a place for everyone without exception. The word 'church' is not synonymous with meetings or buildings. It refers to a group of people who are united together in love and purpose, and joined to Jesus. The church is to be united together and can thus be compared to one human body.

When everyone is seated together in this way, prepare the whole body to answer questions such as: Who are you? Everyone is to answer together: 'We are the church of God,' or, 'We are the body of Jesus Christ.'

94

The Bible says that if we confess our sins, God will forgive us. He will also transform our characters by changing our unrighteous ways and attitudes by the power of the Holy Spirit (1 Jn 1:9–10). This response gives everyone present an opportunity to confess particular sins and 'throw off everything that hinders and the sin that so easily entangles' (Heb 12:1).

Have enough small pebbles for each individual present to be given one each. Pass them round, and ask each person to take one and hold it in their hand. As they hold it, ask them prayerfully to think of any hindrances to following Jesus that they might be aware of in their life which the stone could represent.

Have a place prepared where everyone who wants to can come forward and leave their stone. The foot of a cross or banner could be used. An empty chair could be appropriate – everyone could be asked to imagine that Jesus himself is sitting there. Some people may want to pray as they leave their stone, so allow plenty of time for this. If desired, a prayer of forgiveness and cleansing could be prayed for each one.

95

Anyone present can make this response if Jesus Christ is their Saviour and Lord and they want this to continue for the rest of their lives, or if they want to commit their lives to Jesus for the first time.

Prepare an empty cardboard box, which can be made to look like a postbox if desired. Give everyone a piece of paper and a pencil and ask anyone who wants to dedicate, rededicate or continue to live their lives for God to come forward and 'post' their names into the box. If desired, this can happen during the singing of an appropriate song.

96

Everyone who belongs to Jesus Christ is called to be a servant to others, and never give up doing good to all (Jn 13:14; Gal 6:9). The Holy Spirit is given to believers to enable this to happen (1 Cor 12:7). This response gives each person an opportunity to identify the particular contribution they can or do make as servants of Jesus Christ.

Lay a large, long piece of paper on the floor, and ask a volunteer to lie down on top of it. Ask for one or two other volunteers to draw around his or her outline and then cut it out. (Do this in advance if time is short.) Attach the cut-out shape onto a door, wall, large window or other suitable piece of furniture. Have a supply of post-it notes available, and give one to each person present. Ask each person to think of a gift, talent or skill that God has given them, and to write it down on their post-it note. Then ask everyone to stick their post-it onto the cut-out body at an appropriate point, such as during the singing of a chosen song or hymn. These are the 'gifts' which God wants each one to use to serve others.

97

Using the same idea, this response gives everyone an opportunity to think of practical ways in which they can help others in the church.

Prepare the life-size cut-out of the body shape, give each person a post-it note and ask them to write on it something practical they could do to serve another church member during the following week (Heb 6:10). Then everyone is to stick their post-its onto the cut-out body in the same way.

98

Using the same idea, this response gives everyone an opportunity to think of practical ways they can help others in their neighbourhoods.

Prepare a cut-out body shape in the same way, or instead, display a large map of the local area. Give out post-it notes and ask everyone to write onto their post-it a practical way in which they will serve or help someone who is not a member of the church during the following week. 'As we have opportunity, let us do good to all people' (Gal 6:10). Again, once everyone has finished writing, ask them to stick their post-its onto the body shape or the map.

99

Serving others is a way of life which all Christians should be exhorted to follow. This is a practical response to the instructions of Jesus.

Jesus said in John 13:14–17 that we should follow his example and wash one another's feet (or, in today's world, be prepared to lay aside our pride and dignity and serve one another).

In advance, prepare bowls half-filled with water. (Cereal bowls are perfectly adequate, as not much water is required.) Place them on tables which are conveniently situated. Two sheets of kitchen roll should be laid by each bowl. Explain how Jesus washed the feet of his disciples, and how this necessary task would have been the most menial in society at that time. Culturally, this is not an appropriate picture of servanthood for us, but we can still understand its meaning and significance. It is easier with our Western style of dress to wash one another's hands rather than one another's feet. Ask everyone to think of someone present whose hands they would like to wash in the same servant manner that Jesus had when he washed his disciples' feet. Ask them to fetch one of the bowls of water and the kitchen roll sheets and take them to that person and wash and dry their hands.

100

Jesus said how important it was for his followers to be people who put his commandments into practice. What is the point of knowing all about them and not doing what they say (Mt 7:24–27)? This response engages everyone in an agreement to apply the words they have been listening to.

At the end of a talk or exhortation, ask the people if they agree with what has been said. If the feeling is generally 'yes', ask everyone to repeat after you a suitable verbal commitment. The right words will be needed for the particular situation, but here is an example: 'We are the members of . . . Church. We will continue to live our lives believing in Jesus Christ as commanded in the Scriptures. We will continue to meet together as commanded in the Scriptures. We will continue to love each other as commanded in the Scriptures. We will continue to do good to everyone as commanded in the Scriptures.'

If desired, a suitable verbal commitment can be agreed together using an OHP to record sentences of response which are suggested by the congregation. Once agreed, everyone can read aloud together.

100 Instant Children's Talks

by Sue Relf

- When you need an idea fast…
- When you need a visual aid instantly…
- When you need a song suggestion now…

…you need this book – 100 simple, practical talks for use in primary schools, Sunday schools or family services.

Kingsway Publications

100 Instant Faith-Sharing Talks

by Ian Knox

Here are essential guidelines on how to talk about your faith, together with 100 outline talks for every occasion, including:

- women's meetings
- youth gatherings
- social evenings
- men's breakfasts
- church meetings
- family services

'Ian Knox is a fine evangelist who has devoted his life to making Christ known. May these fruits of his ministry inspire us all to be better communicators of the best news of all.'
                                    – *George Carey, Archbishop of Canterbury*

Kingsway Publications

100 Simple Bible Craft Ideas for Children

by Sue Price

Many of us learn more effectively when we have something to see and something to make; when we can interact rather than simply sit and listen.

Crafts can therefore be used as a vital part of any session with children, and not just an add-on. This collection of illustrated ideas has been specifically designed to help children learn stories and truths from the Bible in such a way that they can make them part of their lives. They are ideal for teachers who would not regard themselves as experts, yet can easily be adapted by the more experienced!

The ideas have been grouped according to categories:

- Bible stories
- Lesson reminders
- Aids to worship
- Crafts to give
- Seasonal items

 Kingsway Publications

100 Creative Prayer Ideas for Children

by Jan Dyer

Children are made in the image of a Creator God, and they enjoy being creative themselves! So it makes sense to use a variety of ways to stimulate children to develop their prayer lives. That way they can build a meaningful friendship with him that will last a lifetime.

Jan Dyer has provided an array of tried and tested ideas, divided into ten areas of a child's life. And a host of 'Additional Ideas' provide even more ways to make prayer a creative and rewarding activity for the children in your care.

 Kingsway Publications

50 Five Minute Stories

by Lynda Neilands

'Please tell us a story...'

You have been asked to fill the next five or ten
minutes with a story. You want something that will
hold the children's attention and stay in their minds.
A story that will give the adults something to think
about. You need fresh ideas, parables, true stories,
once-upon-a-time stories. This book is for you!

Kingsway Publications

50 Stories for Special Occasions

by Lynda Neilands

Good stories teach values, touch the emotions, foster empathy, lodge in the memory and can be a powerful vehicle for spiritual truth.

This is a book of stories for telling to children. Divided into sections, one for each month of the year, here you will find stories appropriate for:

- Christmas
- Easter, Harvest
- Valentine's Day
- Mothering Sunday
- Bible Sunday
- Father's Day

…and many more!

Each story is accompanied by an application, teaching point, Bible reading and a list of relevant songs.

 Kingsway Publications

Learning Styles

by Marlene LeFever

We know that people are different, yet so often we expect them to learn in the same way. They don't. Some respond well to our traditional teaching methods, while others struggle. Some need to talk in order to learn. Others learn best when they can move and learn at the same time. Still others remember pictures more than words. There is no 'right' way.

This book identifies four learning styles that form a Natural Learning Cycle. It shows how to involve *every* person being taught, young and old. Different students will come to the fore at different times in the lesson, depending on the basic question they are asking:

- Why do I need to know this? (*'Imaginative'*)
- What are the facts? (*'Analytic'*)
- How will it work? (*'Common sense'*)
- How can I develop what I have learned? (*'Dynamic'*)

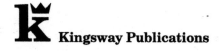 **Kingsway Publications**